D0577166

That Advanced
Industry and
Technology

For a free color catalog describing Gareth Stevens Publishing's list of high-quality books and multimedia programs, call 1-800-542-2595 (USA) or 1-800-461-9120 (Canada). Gareth Stevens Publishing's Fax: (414) 332-3567.

The editor would like to extend thanks to Randy Farchmin, science instructor, Milwaukee Area Technical College, Milwaukee, Wisconsin, for his kind and professional help with the information in this book.

Library of Congress Cataloging-in-Publication Data

Casanellas, Antonio.
    [Industria y la tecnologia. English]
    Great discoveries and inventions that advanced industry and technology / by Antonio Casanellas; illustrated by Ali Garousi.
        p. cm. — (Great discoveries and inventions)
    Includes bibliographical references and index.
    Summary: Describes the invention and function of such things as a combine harvester, a laser, an electron microscope, a missile, and plastic. Includes several related activities.
    ISBN 0-8368-2583-7 (lib. bdg.)
    1. Inventions—Juvenile literature. 2. Technology—Juvenile literature. [1. Inventions. 2. Technology.] I. Garousi, Ali, ill. II. Title. III. Series.
T48. C37413   2000
609—dc21   99-053264

First published in North America in 2000 by
Gareth Stevens Publishing
A World Almanac Education Group Company
330 West Olive Street, Suite 100
Milwaukee, WI 53212 USA

This U.S. edition © 2000 by Gareth Stevens, Inc. Original edition © 1999 by Ediciones Lema, S.L., Barcelona, Spain. Translated from the Spanish by Chantal Ducoeurjoly. Photographic composition and photo mechanics: Novasis, S.A.L., Barcelona (Spain). Additional end matter © 2000 by Gareth Stevens, Inc.

Printed in the United States of America

1 2 3 4 5 6 7 8 9 04 03 02 01 00

Gareth Stevens Publishing
A WORLD ALMANAC EDUCATION GROUP COMPANY

Digging Machines

Have you ever seen huge digging machines at work? Most of them are loader backhoes. They easily excavate earth and load it into trucks. The loader backhoe, as shown below, was invented in 1957 by J. I. Case. The machine works by a system of levers, operated by hydraulic rams. A liquid called hydraulic fluid moves the ram, a piston inside a cylinder. The movement of the piston carries along the part of the loader backhoe to which it is attached.

Loader backhoes have a front loading bucket to scoop material, to level earth, or to load things into trucks. They also have a backhoe to excavate deep holes.

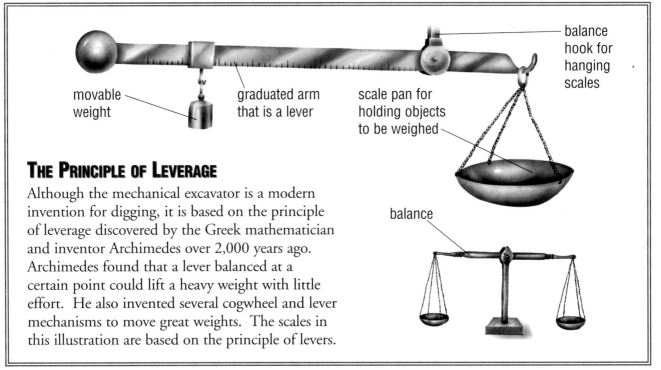

balance hook for hanging scales

movable weight

graduated arm that is a lever

scale pan for holding objects to be weighed

balance

THE PRINCIPLE OF LEVERAGE

Although the mechanical excavator is a modern invention for digging, it is based on the principle of leverage discovered by the Greek mathematician and inventor Archimedes over 2,000 years ago. Archimedes found that a lever balanced at a certain point could lift a heavy weight with little effort. He also invented several cogwheel and lever mechanisms to move great weights. The scales in this illustration are based on the principle of levers.

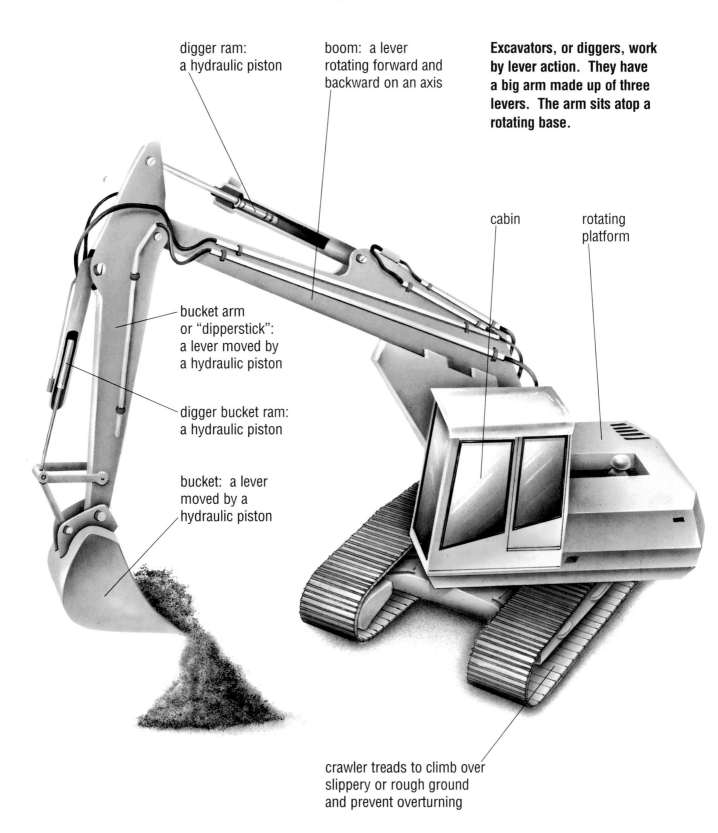

digger ram:
a hydraulic piston

boom: a lever
rotating forward and
backward on an axis

**Excavators, or diggers, work
by lever action. They have
a big arm made up of three
levers. The arm sits atop a
rotating base.**

cabin

rotating
platform

bucket arm
or "dipperstick":
a lever moved by
a hydraulic piston

digger bucket ram:
a hydraulic piston

bucket: a lever
moved by a
hydraulic piston

crawler treads to climb over
slippery or rough ground
and prevent overturning

The Combine Harvester

In earlier times, farmers harvested their wheat by hand. They cut it with scythes and threshed it by beating the grains from the straw. Today, this system of getting in a large crop is rarely used. The invention of the combine harvester revolutionized grain harvesting. It is called a "combine" because it combines the functions of harvesting and threshing into one machine. The combine cuts the wheat and moves it with a system of augers, or huge screws, to mechanical beaters and screens that separate the grain from the straw. The machine can bag the grain or load it directly into trucks. The empty straw is scattered onto the field.

The combine harvester, like the one in this illustration, is based on Archimedes' screw. Inside, a series of big augers, or screws, carries the grain through the steps of threshing and cleaning. The wheat comes directly out of some machines in bags. Other machines use a spout to blow the loose grain into trucks.

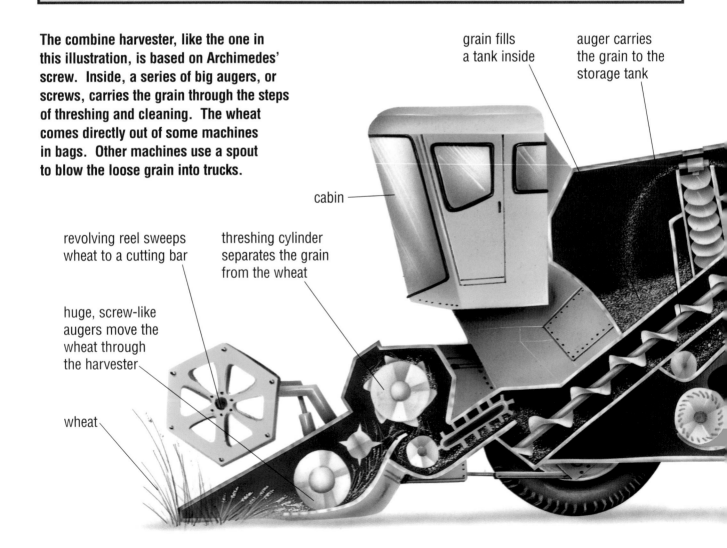

grain fills a tank inside

auger carries the grain to the storage tank

cabin

revolving reel sweeps wheat to a cutting bar

threshing cylinder separates the grain from the wheat

huge, screw-like augers move the wheat through the harvester

wheat

ARCHIMEDES' SCREW

As you can see in the main illustration on these pages, several large screws, called augers, inside the combine harvester move wheat through the steps of cutting, threshing, and cleaning. The combine harvester is a modern invention, but it is based on the principle of the screw that Archimedes discovered over 2,000 years ago. Big augers are still used to transfer water for irrigation *(right)*. When the screw is turned, the lower part of the screw's thread rises, bringing water into the spiral. The moving spiral carries water up to a canal that takes the water to the fields.

The combine harvester greatly reduces the work of harvesting. Years ago, harvesting was done by many farmers working together. Today, only one of these machines is needed to do the job.

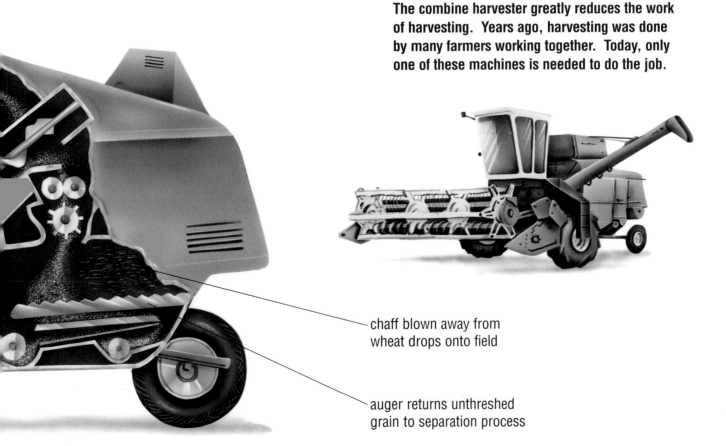

chaff blown away from wheat drops onto field

auger returns unthreshed grain to separation process

Thermoelectric Power Station

Thermoelectric power stations use heat to generate electricity. The heat is produced by burning fossil fuels, such as oil or coal, or by using nuclear reactors to turn water into steam. The steam pushes against the blades and vanes of a turbine, spinning it. The moving turbine rotates the shaft of the generator, which produces electricity. The electricity then goes to a transformer that changes the voltage and sends the electricity into the power grid's supply for distribution to homes and industries.

THERMOELECTRIC POWER STATION

Well over half of the electricity needed for homes and industries is generated in power stations like the one shown here. Some of these stations have the capacity to generate over a million kilowatts of electricity.

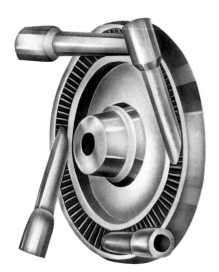

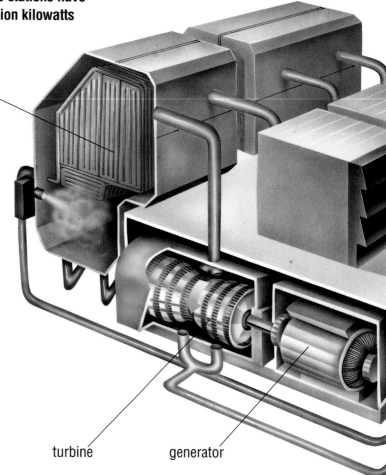

boiler

turbine   generator

POWER STATION TURBINES

The turbines are made up of cylindrical housings containing angled blades *(above)*. Steam pushes against the blades to turn the central shaft that runs the generator.

MODEL STEAM ENGINE

Nearly 2,000 years ago, Hero of Alexandria, a Greek inventor, used a model to demonstrate the principle of steam power. The model consisted of a hollow ball held by two tubes connected to a water container. Underneath, a fire boiled the water to produce steam. The steam rose through the tubes and pushed against the ball to turn it. Practical steam engines could not be made until stronger metals were developed later.

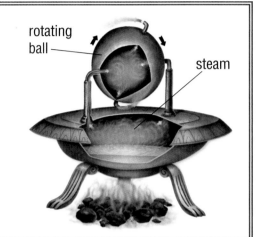

rotating ball

steam

cooling tower

TURBINE BLADES

In this illustration *(below)*, you see a steam turbine.

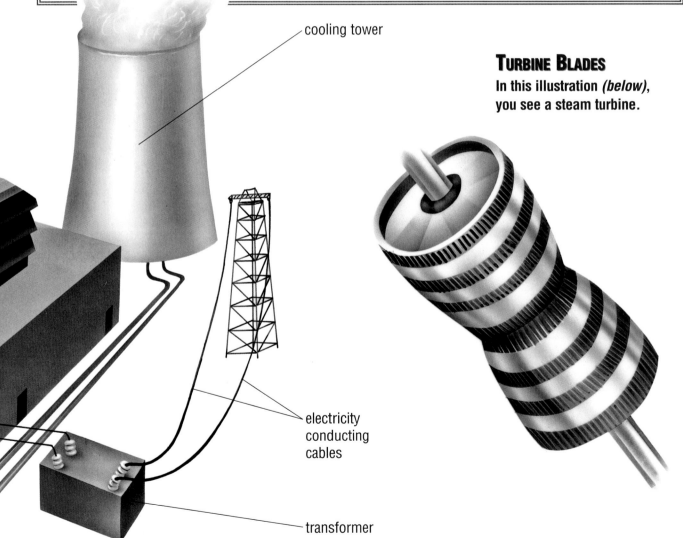

electricity conducting cables

transformer

The Microscope

Magnifying lenses made in the fifteenth and sixteenth centuries were mainly toys for the curious wealthy. In the mid-seventeenth century, Antoni van Leeuwenhoek, in the Netherlands, built microscopes with a single, powerful lens that magnified up to 270 times. He was the first to see blood cells, single-celled animals, and bacteria. Two hundred years later, more powerful microscopes, with changeable focus and light controls, allowed researchers to develop the science of bacteriology. Today, microscopes using electrons, instead of light, can enlarge images a million times — much larger than the magnification of two thousand times possible with light microscopes. Scientists using electron microscopes can see and study viruses, details of cell structure, and other minute objects.

HOW DOES A MICROSCOPE WORK?

The compound light microscope has lenses in two places. The objective lens, at the bottom of the tube, magnifies the specimen on the stage. The ocular lens, at the top of the tube, magnifies this enlarged image. To find the total magnification, multiply the power of both lenses. For example, an ocular with a power of 10, times an objective with the power of 80 (10 × 80), produces an image 800 times its natural size. A rotating turret with three or four objective lenses offers several powers, or strengths, of magnification. A mirror reflects light through the specimen. Most modern microscopes have two oculars at the top, one for each eye, and an electric lamp under the stage. A light condenser intensifies the light entering the lenses.

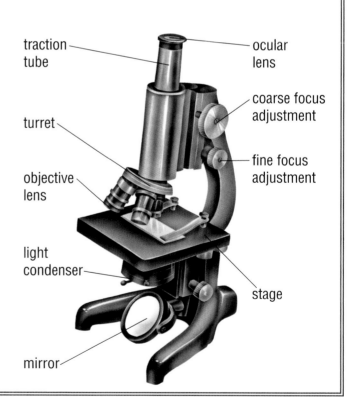

9

Seeing with Electrons

The diagram below shows how an electron microscope sends a beam of electrons through the specimen to be magnified. Magnetic lenses focus the beam. The enlarged image of the object appears on a viewing screen.

Different 'Scopes

Some electron microscopes, like the one below, can show molecules. Scanning electron microscopes can produce a three-dimensional picture. Acoustic microscopes use sound waves to create images.

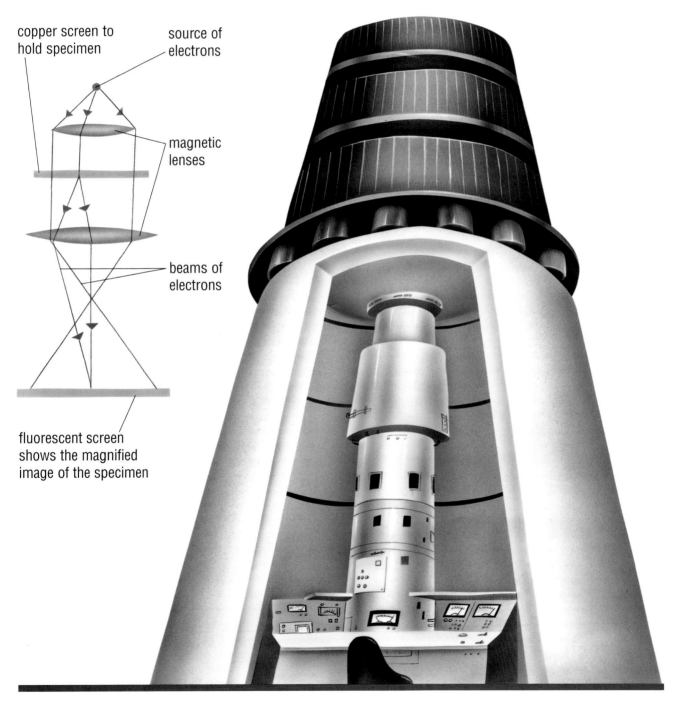

copper screen to hold specimen

source of electrons

magnetic lenses

beams of electrons

fluorescent screen shows the magnified image of the specimen

Lights and Lasers

Electric light was possible after Thomas Edison invented the light bulb in the late nineteenth century. In 1960, using a ruby rod, Dr. Theodore Maiman made the first laser. A laser is a beam of light that doesn't spread and dim, as ordinary light does. Instead, it can travel a long way in a powerful, narrow beam. Several materials can make lasers with different properties. Digital recording and fiber optic communications use visible lasers. Invisible infrared laser beams operate cash registers and TV remote controls, and they can cut hard objects, such as metal.

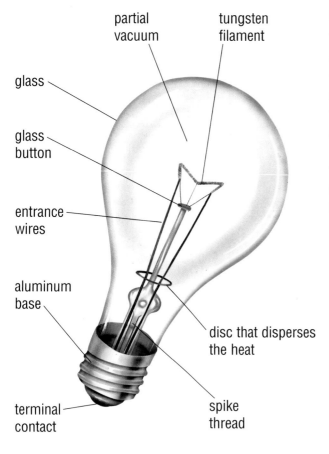

partial vacuum

tungsten filament

glass

glass button

entrance wires

aluminum base

disc that disperses the heat

terminal contact

spike thread

A MODERN ELECTRIC LIGHT BULB

GAS LASER

This gas laser contains helium and neon enclosed in a tube. Electricity supplies power. The gas atoms absorb the energy and release it as laser light. The light travels back and forth between the mirrors and increases in power. When the light becomes strong enough, it bursts through the partially reflecting mirror as a laser beam. All this happens within seconds.

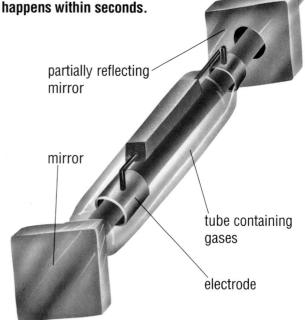

partially reflecting mirror

mirror

tube containing gases

electrode

laser
beam

torch

candle

gas streetlight

LIGHT BEFORE ELECTRICITY

Until the invention of the light bulb, artificial light was obtained from candles or oil lamps. In some cities, gas lamps connected to city pipes. Edison's invention revolutionized society, since it allowed people to have light at their disposal all day and night.

EDISON'S FIRST LIGHT BULB

Edison's first light bulb *(right)* used a carbonized cotton thread. Electricity passed through the carbon, which glowed when it became hot. Most of the air was removed from the bulb to prevent the filament from flaming. Edison soon found that a carbonized bamboo filament would last longer. The hotter a filament becomes, the more light it gives off. Modern bulbs use a thin tungsten wire, which can rise to a temperature approaching 6,170° Fahrenheit (3,410° Celsius) to produce a very bright light. A light bulb filament must be enclosed in a partial vacuum or an inert gas, such as argon, to prevent it from catching fire in oxygen. Fused-quartz tubes can now be used in place of the glass light bulb.

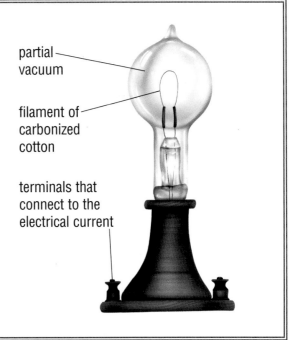

partial
vacuum

filament of
carbonized
cotton

terminals that
connect to the
electrical current

Telecommunications

For thousands of years, people could only communicate short distances, using flags or other visual signals and bells or other sounds. In the eighteenth century, the telegraph was invented to send messages through wires. Later, Guglielmo Marconi perfected the wireless, or radio, telegraph. Today, radio signals link the world, mostly through communication satellites.

A communication satellite moves at a speed that keeps it high above the same spot on the rotating Earth's equator. Because it appears not to move, it is said to be geostationary. Communication satellites are linked to one another, making it possible to send signals over long distances. Stations on Earth transmit and receive the satellite signals.

The communication satellite *(left)*, in its geostationary position above Earth, receives signals from a broadcasting antenna and transmits them to receiving antennae based at points on Earth *(below)*.

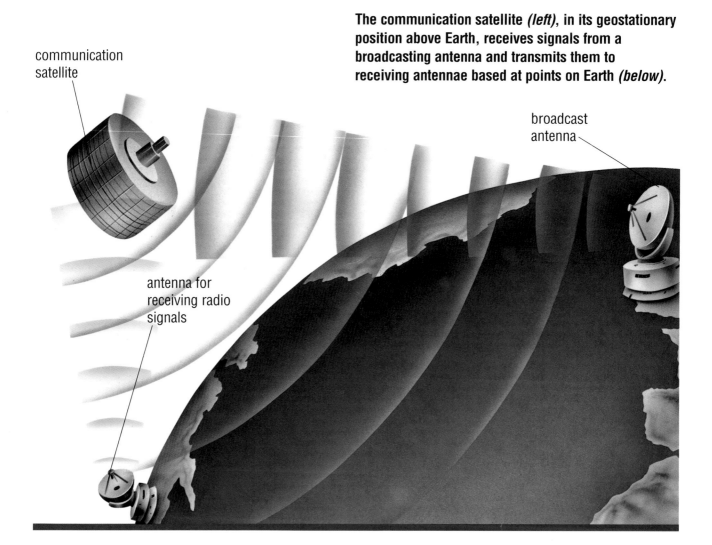

communication satellite

broadcast antenna

antenna for receiving radio signals

Big parabolic, or curved, antennae transmit signals. They send signals in only one direction.

Communication satellites are geostationary. They move in an orbit at a speed that keeps them over the same fixed point above Earth's equator. It takes several satellites to cover the entire surface of the planet.

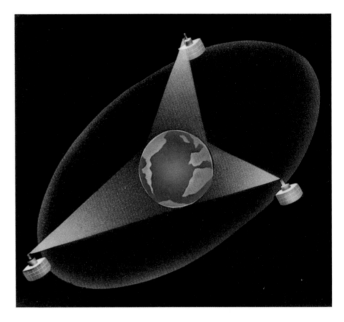

THE MARCONI TELEGRAPH

The telegraph was developed by several inventors who made important contributions. At the end of the last century, Guglielmo Marconi improved an earlier invention, making telegraphs that transmitted messages through radio waves rather than through wires or cables. In the Marconi telegraph *(right)*, the antenna was a metal plate that sent electromagnetic radio waves. The wireless telegraph was very useful for sending Morse code messages to boats or trains because the wireless telegraph could send radio messages without connecting cables.

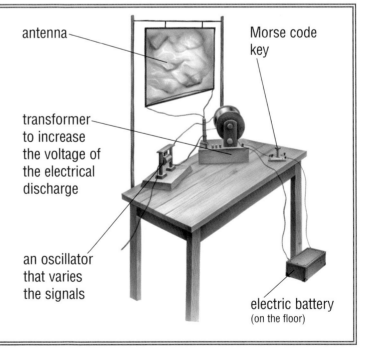

antenna

Morse code key

transformer to increase the voltage of the electrical discharge

an oscillator that varies the signals

electric battery
(on the floor)

Missiles

Missiles are self-propelled rockets. They carry either solid or liquid fuel and oxygen for internal combustion. Because they are self-contained, missiles can operate in the vacuum of space. Rocket missiles can launch satellites into orbit. Some missiles are guided by remote control. Others are self-guided, using inertial guidance systems that detect motion. Inertially guided missiles can correct their own flight paths. Missiles fired from Earth's surface follow a curved path called a parabola. Multistage missiles drop stages as the fuel is used up.

GUIDED MISSILE

Some air-to-surface missiles, like the one below, incorporate a television guidance system.

television camera

BALLISTIC MISSILE

A ballistic missile, fired from Earth's surface, takes a parabolic flight path.

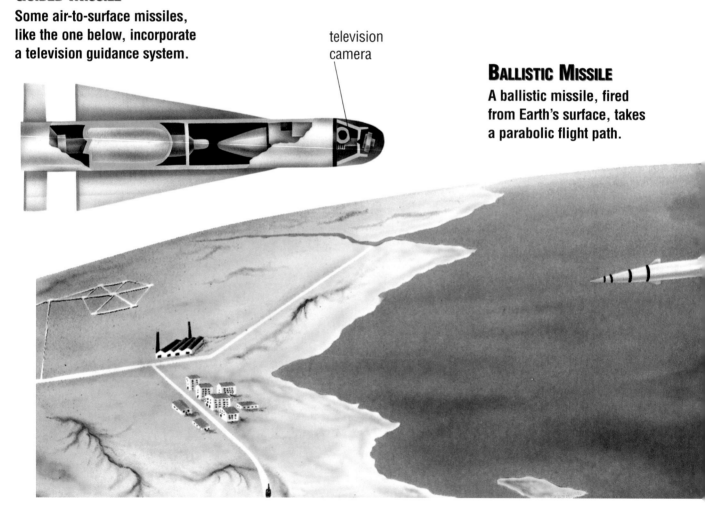

Parabolic Flight Paths

Galileo Galilei studied the laws governing
the flight paths of artillery projectiles, such
as cannonballs. Up to then, scientists
thought that a launched body followed two
straight paths, angling straight upward and
then straight downward, as shown at right.
Galileo proved that when an object is
projected, or shot out, it travels in a parabola,
a type of curve. This discovery established
the groundwork for ballistics, the science
of projectile paths.

Long-Range Missiles

**This long-range missile has a gyroscope on
board to detect motion and make corrections.**

inertial guidance system
using motion detectors

radar

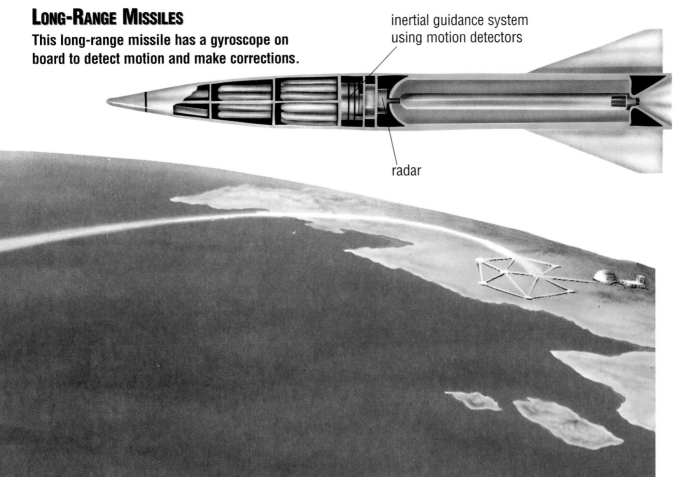

The Modern Paper Mill

Ancient Egyptians made an early form of paper from papyrus, a plant. Europeans wrote on thin sheepskin called parchment. The Chinese invented true paper about 105 A.D. In the eighth century, Middle Easterners learned the process, and in Spain in 1150, they built a paper mill that made a sheet at a time from rags. Modern machines grind wood and mix it with water and chemicals to make pulp. Adding other chemicals makes different kinds of paper. The pulp is spread on a fast-moving screen, where suction removes the water. The paper is pressed, dried on hot rollers, and cut to a final shape. Rag paper is also still made.

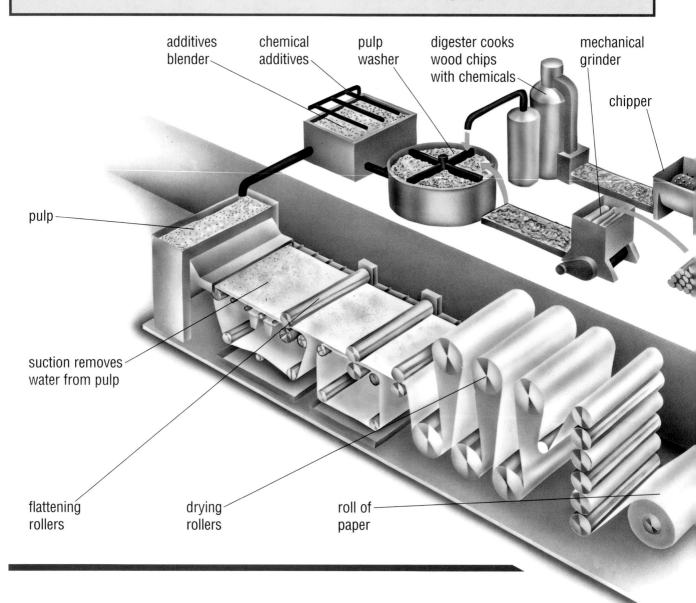

additives blender
chemical additives
pulp washer
digester cooks wood chips with chemicals
mechanical grinder
chipper
pulp
suction removes water from pulp
flattening rollers
drying rollers
roll of paper

EARLY PAPERMAKING

In early paper mills, paper was made from rags. They were wet and allowed to rot to loosen the fibers. These were then cooked in lime, ground up, washed, and bleached in the sun. The floating pieces of pulp were suspended in water and scooped up by a hand-held, framed screen. This was shaken as the water drained, making a wet mat. The mats were stacked between felt sheets, pressed, and hung up to dry. The process was slow, and paper was scarce. Today, the use of wood gives us a large supply of inexpensive paper. But rags still make the best quality paper.

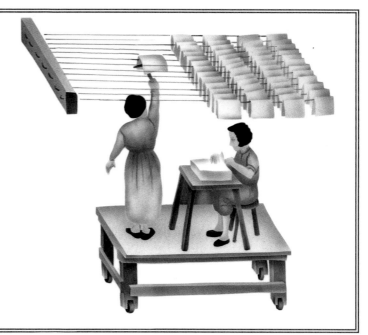

MODERN PAPER MILL

Modern papermaking is shown at left. The top track shows pulp made by digesting wood with heat and chemicals. Just under this is shown the cold, ground-wood process of making paper pulp.

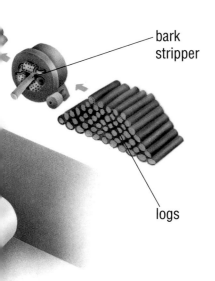

bark stripper

logs

EASTERN PAPERMAKING

In China, paper was made from mulberry bark. Later, Chinese papermakers in Central Asia used flax and hemp. From China, papermaking spread to the Middle East.

Particle Accelerator

Matter is made up of atoms, but for a long time scientists had differing ideas about how atoms were built. In 1895, Sir Joseph Thomson discovered electrons. Early in the 1900s, researchers used particles from natural radioactive sources, such as radium, to study the atom's parts. They discovered the nucleus and, later, the proton and neutron that make it up.

In the 1930s, Ernest O. Lawrence built his cyclotron, the first frying pan-sized particle accelerator. It used magnetic fields to speed up streams of particles to collide with atoms and split their nuclei. This led to today's colliders that are miles wide. By studying the results of the collisions, scientists continue to discover more subatomic particles, such as quarks.

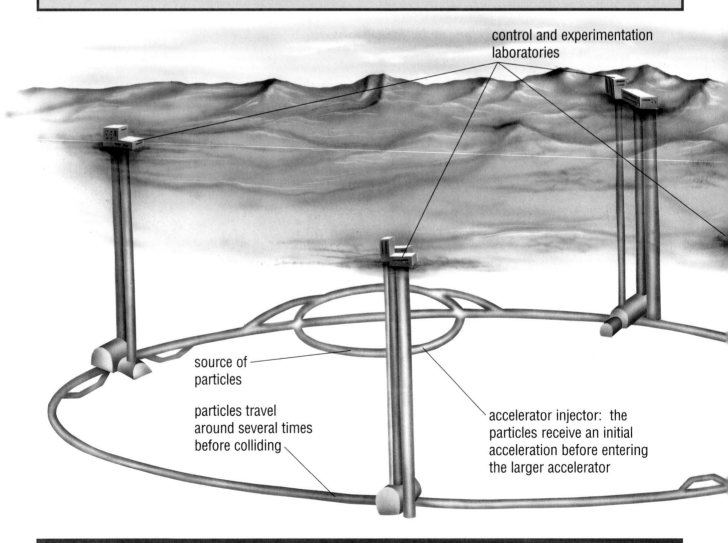

control and experimentation laboratories

source of particles

particles travel around several times before colliding

accelerator injector: the particles receive an initial acceleration before entering the larger accelerator

THE ATOMIC NUCLEUS

In 1911, Ernest Rutherford used a radium gun *(right)* to shoot natural alpha particles at sheets of gold. Some particles shot back instead of going through the gold. This revealed the presence of a dense core in the gold atoms. He called the core the nucleus. He later found the proton. Several years later, the neutron was discovered. Neutrons and protons make up an atom's nucleus. Today, high-speed particle accelerators continue to reveal subatomic particles.

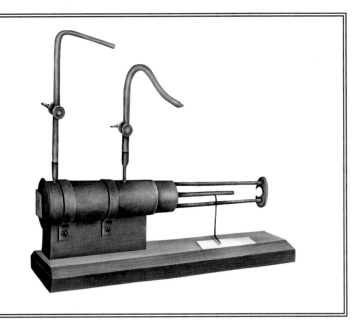

PARTICLE ACCELERATOR
The particle accelerator uses magnetic force to speed up millions of particles so that they are fast enough to split the nuclei of atoms.

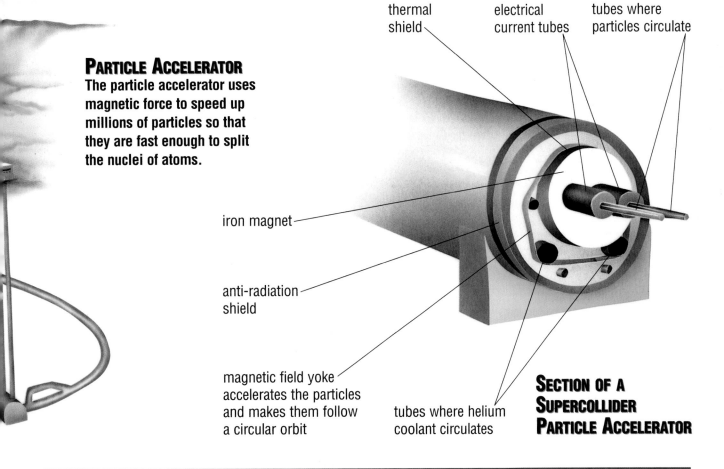

thermal shield

electrical current tubes

tubes where particles circulate

iron magnet

anti-radiation shield

magnetic field yoke accelerates the particles and makes them follow a circular orbit

tubes where helium coolant circulates

SECTION OF A SUPERCOLLIDER PARTICLE ACCELERATOR

Plastics

Early plastics made in the nineteenth century, such as celluloid and casein, were made from plant fibers and milk curds. Early plastics could be molded and shaped. But celluloid burned easily, and casein cracked when cold. The first plastic using substances humans made was Bakelite in 1909. It was molded into objects or used to make varnishes and other coatings. The use of Bakelite quickly spread into other industries, such as the manufacture of electrical fittings and automobiles. Plastics are made from organic chemicals, which contain carbon atoms. These molecules are joined into very long chains, which give plastics properties of flexibility and long life. Most plastics are now made from petroleum. Plastic can be shaped in more ways than can any other material.

hopper for plastic granules

During manufacture, plastics release toxic chemicals into the air and water. This causes acid rain, which damages the environment *(above)*. Plastic items disintegrate extremely slowly, so they crowd our landfills. When carelessly discarded, plastics can injure wild animals. The plastics industry continues to search for ways to control these problems.

ORGANIC CHEMISTRY

Organic chemistry studies carbon compounds. Scientists once believed that organic chemicals only existed in substances that came from living things. But now a multitude of products, such as plastics and medicines, are produced with artificial carbon compounds. Carbon atoms combine with each other in a way that makes large chains. By recombining these, an infinite variety of differing compounds can be made.

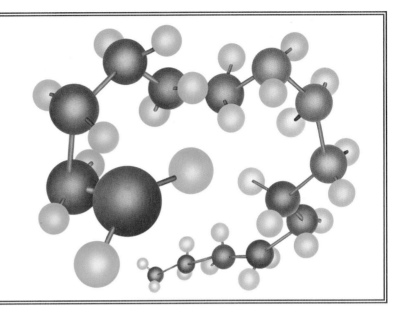

COMPRESSION MOLDING

At right, plastic is heat-formed into hollow shapes by a two-part mold.

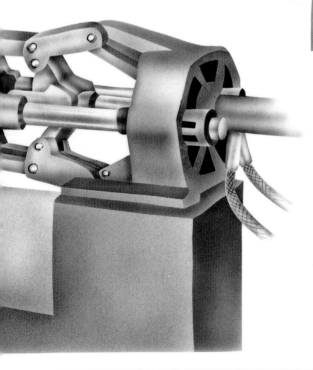

1. plastic granules

2. heated item

3. finished item

INJECTION MOLDING

Raw plastic is formed as granules that can be manufactured into many items. At left, an injection molder is used to make solid items. A hopper feeds plastic granules into the machine, where the plastic is heated and injected into a mold. Later, the item is removed from the mold.

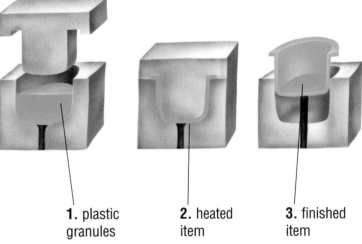

PROJECT

Expanding Force

YOU WILL NEED:

straight pin

deep dish with hot water

bottle with cool water and airtight stopper

air-drying clay

modeling clay

drinking straw

When water inside a container boils, it produces steam. The expanding steam presses strongly against the inside walls of the container. This pressure can be used to perform work. This is what happens inside a thermoelectric station. The expanding steam is used to turn turbines that generate electricity. This project will show you the force of expansion. Instead of steam, it uses warming air.

1. Fill the bottle halfway with cool water.

2. Make a small hole in the stopper. Ask an adult to help you.

3. Push the stopper into the bottle, and push the drinking straw through the hole in the stopper, as shown in illustration 3.

4. Cover the space around the straw with modeling clay.

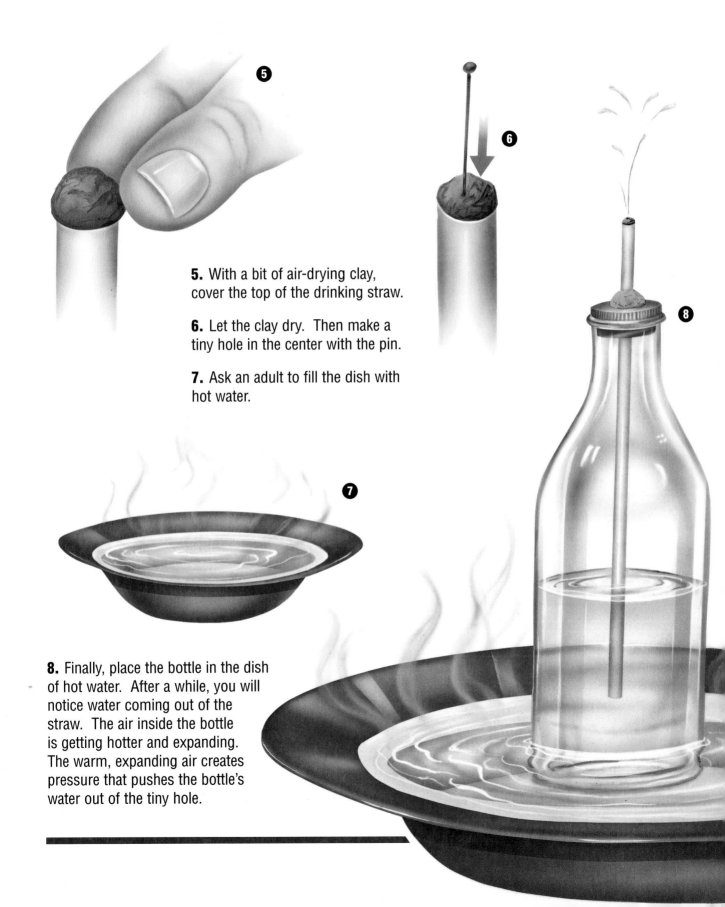

5. With a bit of air-drying clay, cover the top of the drinking straw.

6. Let the clay dry. Then make a tiny hole in the center with the pin.

7. Ask an adult to fill the dish with hot water.

8. Finally, place the bottle in the dish of hot water. After a while, you will notice water coming out of the straw. The air inside the bottle is getting hotter and expanding. The warm, expanding air creates pressure that pushes the bottle's water out of the tiny hole.

Generating Life

YOU WILL NEED:

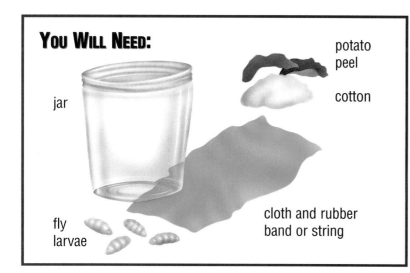

jar

potato peel

cotton

fly larvae

cloth and rubber band or string

People of an earlier time believed that flies and worms started their lives in rotting substances by "spontaneous generation," or just instantly appearing. The microscope revealed that these little creatures actually came from tiny eggs, showing that "life comes from life." This is now a basic biological principle. In this project, you can demonstrate this fact studied by microbiologists.

①

1. In a fishing tackle shop, buy some fly larvae and put them inside the jar along with a potato peel and damp cotton.

2. Put the jar in a dark place, well away from any light.

②

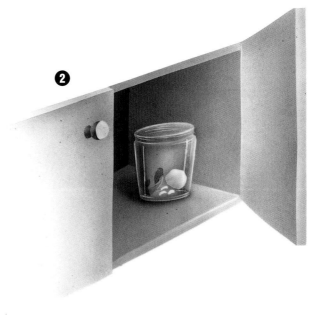

3. A few days later, you will find that the larvae are getting darker. Take them out and change the potato peel and the cotton.

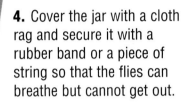

4. Cover the jar with a cloth rag and secure it with a rubber band or a piece of string so that the flies can breathe but cannot get out.

5. After a few days, adult flies will emerge.

6. A few days later, these flies will lay eggs from which more fly larvae will develop.

Origami: A Paper Swan

YOU WILL NEED:

square sheets
of paper

The paper that is made in modern paper factories is not used only for printing newspapers. It can also be used in the Japanese art of origami. Simply by folding pieces of paper, you can construct a variety of miniature objects, such as boats, planes, and animals. With this project, you can create one of these paper objects. Try making one of the most well-known of the origami figures — the paper swan. Fold carefully.

1. Take a square piece of paper and fold it along the diagonal — from corner to corner.

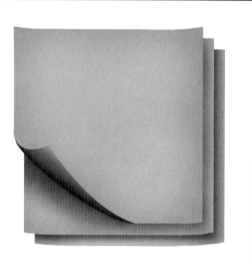

2

3. Fold each outside corner inward so that its whole side of the square touches the center fold line.

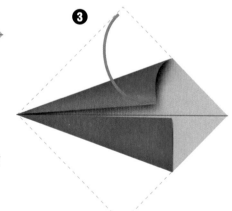

2. Flatten the paper again. Now you have the center fold line.

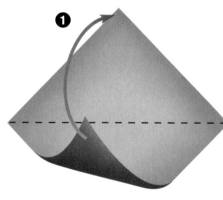

4. Again, fold the new outside corners inward to touch the center fold line.

5. Your paper will have this thin, pointed shape.

6. Fold your whole shape along the first center fold line so that the two "backs" of your shape touch each other.

7. You will fold the point of your shape back over the "body" along the dotted line *(as shown)* to form the swan's neck.

8. Fold the neck up so that it tilts a little back from being straight up and down.

9. Fold the top point down over the neck to form the swan's head and beak. Using tempera paints, color your swan as you like. You can make more swans to form a group or to give as gifts to your friends.

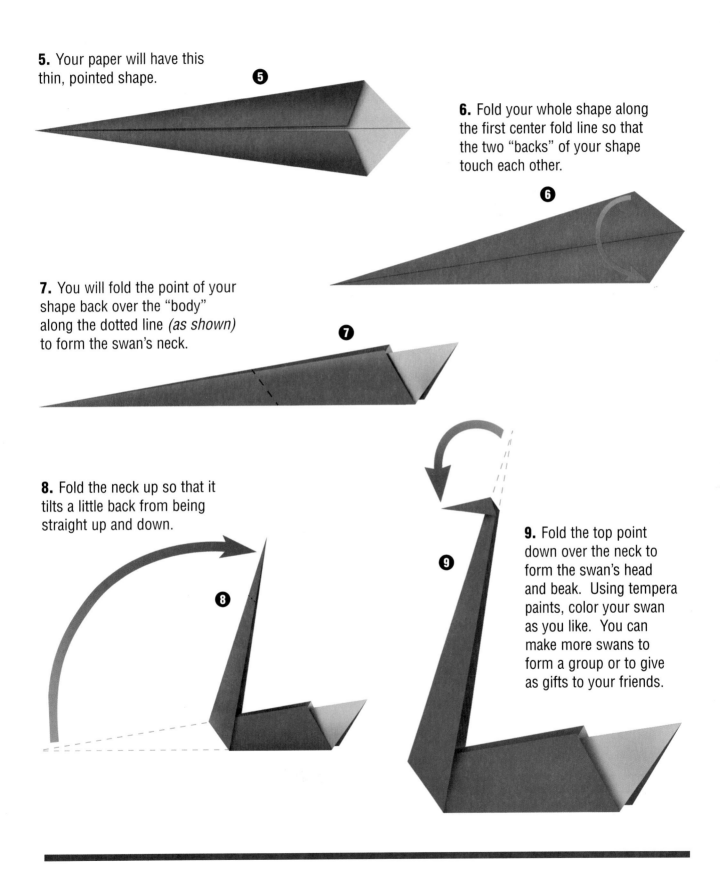

PROJECT

How an Atom Splits

YOU WILL NEED:

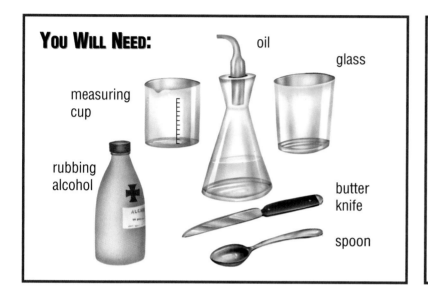

measuring cup

oil

glass

rubbing alcohol

butter knife

spoon

The division of an atom is called fission. Today's high-speed particle accelerators rupture, or break, atoms into increasingly smaller components, or parts. Early researchers learned how to split an atom of one element into atoms of different elements. When an atom splits in this way, it acts similarly to a drop of liquid dividing into two parts. This project demonstrates one way in which an atom can act when split.

1. With the measuring cup, measure one part water and two parts alcohol. Pour both liquids into the glass.

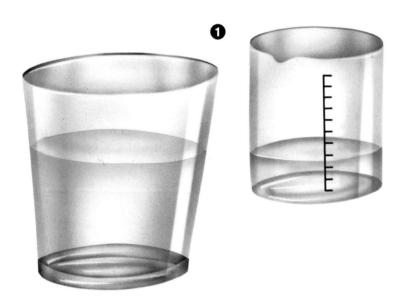

❶

❷

2. With the spoon, stir the mixture well.

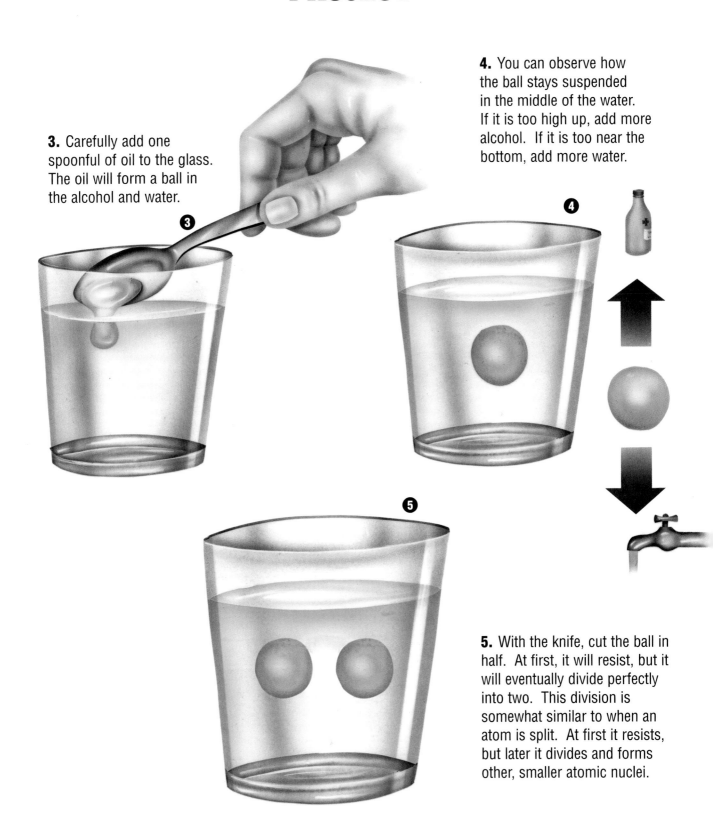

3. Carefully add one spoonful of oil to the glass. The oil will form a ball in the alcohol and water.

4. You can observe how the ball stays suspended in the middle of the water. If it is too high up, add more alcohol. If it is too near the bottom, add more water.

5. With the knife, cut the ball in half. At first, it will resist, but it will eventually divide perfectly into two. This division is somewhat similar to when an atom is split. At first it resists, but later it divides and forms other, smaller atomic nuclei.

Glossary

acid rain: precipitation containing pollutants that make it acidic. Acid rain causes damage to the environment and to structures that people have made.

Archimedes' screw: a device made of a large screw inside a cylinder and turned with a hand crank to lift water to a higher level, for example, to an irrigation canal. These are still used to raise water in Egypt.

atom: the smallest part of an element that can exist by itself or in combination with other atoms. Atoms are made up of protons, neutrons, and electrons.

ballistics: the science of the path and motion of projectiles, such as thrown balls.

electrons: negatively charged particles of electricity. One or more electrons orbit an atom's nucleus.

fiber optics: plastic filaments that conduct light and are used to view inside bodies.

filament: a very thin, thread-like structure.

generator: a machine with an iron core wrapped in copper wire that rotates in a magnetic field to create a flow of electricity.

geostationary: the position of a satellite that travels above the equator at the same speed Earth rotates so as to stay above the same place on Earth.

helium: a light, colorless, non-flammable gas found in natural gas, used to inflate airships and balloons and for cooling.

hydraulic: operated by the resistance offered by the pressure of a liquid forced through a tube.

hydraulic piston: a cylindrical piece of metal that moves back and forth in a tube according to the pressure of a liquid.

laser: a device that strengthens light and makes it shine in a very narrow beam; the shortened version of "Light Amplification by Stimulated Emission of Radiation."

lever: a simple machine that aids in the lifting of weight. A crowbar is an example of a lever.

loader backhoe: a machine using hydraulic levers to operate a front bucket for picking up and a backhoe for digging.

Morse code: a system of dots and dashes devised by Samuel Morse in 1838 and used to send messages by sound or light.

neon: a colorless, odorless gas found in minute quantities in air. Neon is used mainly in lamps and signs.

ocular: done or seen by the eye, or having to do with eyes; also, the microscope lens nearest to the eye.

parabola: the curve that a projectile follows after being launched.

petroleum: crude oil taken from the ground. Petroleum is processed into many products, including plastics.

satellite: an object that orbits another object. Communication and data-gathering satellites orbit Earth.

scythe: a tool with a long, curved, and sharp blade attached to a wooden handle. Scythes are used for cutting grain or grass.

threshing: the process of separating grain crops into straw and grain, or seeds.

transformer: an electrical device to raise electricity's voltage for transmission from the power plant and to lower it for home use.

turbine: a device driven by the pressure of water, steam, or air against the curved vanes, or blades, of a wheel.

vacuum: a totally empty space that contains absolutely nothing, including air.

More Books to Read

Airplanes. What If (series). Steve Parker (Copper Beech Books)

The Early Inventions. Jacqueline Dineen and Philip Wilkinson (Chelsea House)

Inventions That Changed Modern Life. Lois Markham (Raintree/Steck Vaughn)

Looking Inside: Machines and Constructions. Paul Fleisher and Patricia Keeler (Atheneum)

Machines. Young Scientist Concepts and Projects (series). Chris Oxlade (Gareth Stevens)

Machines and How They Work. David Burnie (Sterling Publications)

Machines and Inventions. Record Breakers (series). Peter Lafferty (Gareth Stevens)

Satellite Communication. Making Contact (series). Ann Graham Gaines (Smart Apple)

Satellites. 20th Century Inventions (series) Steve Parker (Raintree/Steck Vaughn)

Under the Microscope (series). John Woodward and Casey Horton (Gareth Stevens)

Videos to Watch

Forces: Work and Machines. (Educational Activities)

The Microscope. (Encyclopædia Britannica Educational Corporation)

Paper. (Lucerne Media)

Power from the Atom. (Encyclopædia Britannica Educational Corporation)

There Goes a Bulldozer. (Library Video)

Thomas A. Edison and His Amazing Invention Factories. (Encyclopædia Britannica Educational Corporation)

Web Sites to Visit

www.shu.edu/projects/reals/history/
 archimed.html

www.sciences.demon.co.uk/whistmic.htm

www.thomasedison.com

www.yahooligans.com/Science_and_Nature/
 Machines/Inventions

member.aol.com/jimb3d/

www.historychannel.com/ *(Keyword: plastic)*

Some web sites stay current longer than others. For further web sites, use your search engines to locate the following keywords: *Archimedes, atoms, chemistry, Thomas A. Edison, inventions, lasers, microscopes, paper manufacturing, plastics, telecommunications, thermoelectricity.*

Index